Careen

Carolyn Smart

Careen

Brick Books

Library and Archives Canada Cataloguing in Publication

Smart, Carolyn, author
          Careen / Carolyn Smart.

Issued in print and electronic formats.
ISBN 978-1-77131-382-7 (paperback).—ISBN 978-1-77131-384-1 (pdf).—
ISBN 978-1-77131-383-4 (epub)

          I. Title.

PS8587.M37C37 2015   C811'.54   C2015-903673-9
                                              C2015-903674-7

We acknowledge the Canada Council for the Arts, the Government of Canada
through the Canada Book Fund, and the Ontario Arts Council for their support of
our publishing program.

The author photo was taken by Bernard Clark.
The cover uses a photograph by Roger Palmer.

The book is set in Sabon.
Interior design and layout by Marijke Friesen.
Printed and bound by Sunville Printco Inc.

Brick Books
431 Boler Road, Box 20081
London, Ontario N6K 4G6

www.brickbooks.ca

For Jean, Ingrid, Gillian and Hilary: in-law women

Dreams,
Dreams go on,
Out of the dead on their backs,
Broken and no use any more:
Dreams of the way and the end go on.

— Carl Sandburg, from "Among the Red Guns"

Texas, 1930

starved us off the fields and deafened us with the sawing of insects, the anger and the pungent need

the canyons the gulf plains the coast the lowlands the hill country the basin the range, what do they ask of us now that the soil offers nothing

hear the thin distant whisper of the tribes, the Mound Builders Pueblo Apache Hasinai Comanche, the high singing of the Spaniards the Mexicans, bleached bones along the Rio Grande, the dust of Sam Houston the skull of Zachary Taylor the fallen at the sieges the dead and dying all across the plains

wander the land at night and hear the screech owl lament, crying our history our sad empty fields, how they speak this American shame this endless churning landscape of our fathers who have lost most all they hold dear

come to the cities in your wagons on foot with your mules your women your mangy puling children, cobble whatever shelter you may, tell the old tales mouth the history taste the dust upon your tongue

take flight from one border to another just keep on in the thermal lift and yearn, there are markers of the rivers east and west Pecos Rio Grande Brazos Colorado Red and still we thirst

and the black oil gushing out and out of the spindletops and the strangers who come to town electric chairs in the backrooms and men who throw the switch and the prison farms with lean and beaten men running before the riders with their guns

the miles covered in cars going nowhere but away from here then turning back and back again to the same old gutted roads with faces that stare at you like death is joyriding in the back seat

I

and the blacks all picked up and went somewhere else when the storms blew in there was nothing left behind but the weevil and our gaunt faces peeping out at nothing

now the women's work is over they lie on pallets the lack is another part of breathing and the taste of charity in their mouths and their breasts hanging like pockets of despair

and who remembers now the hurricanes in Indianola and Galveston again in Galveston and the many thousands who died there clutching the Bible to their acquiescent hearts

we walk the streets line the curbs forage in the news lean bewildered against brickwarm walls outrage pooling in our eyes, when will it come, justice and respect, when

into the long white ribbon of road the future careens away

From heart-break some people have suffered
from weariness some people have died.
But take it all in all;
our troubles are small,
till we get like Bonnie and Clyde.

— Bonnie Parker, from "The Trail's End"

Characters

Cumie Barrow: 1874–1942; married Henry Barrow; bore seven children: Elvin, Artie, Marvin (Buck), Nellie, Clyde, L. C. and Marie

Henry Barrow: 1874–1957; sharecropper; married Cumie Walker in 1891

Buck Barrow: 1903–1933; married twice before meeting Blanche Caldwell on Nov. 11, 1929

Blanche Barrow: 1911–1988; married John Callaway 1928 in an arranged marriage; married Buck Barrow 1931; married Eddie Frasure 1940

Clyde Barrow: 1909–1934; known as Bud by his family

Bonnie Parker: 1910–1934; married Roy Thornton 1926; never divorced

L. C. Barrow: 1913–1979; youngest brother of Clyde and Buck Barrow

Marie Barrow: 1918–1999; youngest sister of Clyde and Buck Barrow

W. D. Jones: 1916–1974; son of James and Tookie Jones

Frank Hamer: 1884–1955; Texas Ranger; hired to track down and capture or kill the Barrow Gang following the raid on Eastham Prison Farm

Henry Methvin: 1912–1948; escaped in the Eastham Raid; son of Ivy Methvin

Ivy Methvin: 1885–1946; man who betrayed the gang

Raymond Hamilton: 1913–1935; member of the Barrow Gang at various times

Ralph Fults: 1911–1993; early member of the Barrow Gang

Emery Abernathy: dates unknown, early member of the Barrow Gang

Ross Dyer: dates unknown; a.k.a. Everett Milligan; early member of the Barrow Gang

William Turner: dates unknown, early member of the Barrow Gang

Cumie Barrow

I had one steadfast wish: avoid the idle day.
The devil plays upon a fallow soul.
Also be a helpmeet to my man,
raise the children up right.

Pray. Choose to live within the dust bowl,
sleep beneath the wagon, haul cotton
with ribboned hands.

Not hard to sweep an earthen floor
unless you press your will against the wind,
grains specklin your eyes.

Taught to read but only in the Bible
I grew to read the Gutters about my children,
saw pictures there of widows they made
who wore their bridal clothes to funerals.

It is no lie there was drinkin.
There is only so much room for endless grief.

Few regrets, I'd look forward to the picnics,
red beans and rice, fried chicken in the hand.
Shrill cicadas in evenin light. Listen,

why is my youngest out on the road
past midnight? Patience wears thin as skin,
gunfire all over this land.

A human husk I was, yet fierce til the expected came.
Forgiveness if I did not bend.
Purchased one grave for two loved sons.

Henry Barrow

Ever see a horse run?
Teeth just grindin air, shine
comin off it like a blazin afternoon.
I'd like to get me one.

First day I went to school
I fainted straight down on the ground,
never took to readin, never cared for that.

What good would readin've bin to me?
To read my boys' dark history?
Blood on their heads and hands
and all the weepin in the world
fell down around my head
and in my house.

Only time we found some happiness
we'd just been wed, and then we had but five good years.

Never got no horse,
but went to church and done the proper thing,
married Cumie, she just 16 and under five foot tall.
She was a rock to me all her days.

Started with a rented field
and babies, we had seven.
All lived to tell of hunger, constant movin,
no time left to dream.
Jesus watched us every day.

They called me quiet. True.
I labored til I dropped.
Cumie made the children go to church
and school, she made those younguns mind.
My daddy never hit me
the way her daddy done,
a whippin sets them straight I reckon,
glad it never fell to me.
I was too busy on the journey to provide.

We never had no time to play or watch them grow,
no room for grace
nor kindliness
nor hope.

They grew up, lit out for town,
I worked until my hands were bloody,
I tilled the soil
til cotton root rot come
and weevils et the rotted crop right off.

We moved to Dallas, to the Bog,
started there again.
I was a scrap dealer,
a station owner,
sometimes sold hooch.
Drank some too, some days.
Through illness and the dusty storms
my children did provide for me.

The boys would drive their flashy cars
and dress real well.
They told me all would turn out fine:
they'd buy good land, pasture with some shade,
the things I'd yearned for in this life.

I did not shed a tear
to see them in the ground.
Sat still with Cumie while she mourned,
my head held low
as fits a man without one stroke of luck.

Buck's first run

what I done best was playin outlaw,
maybe I was born one from the get-go.

quit school after third grade, and yeah
I was a happy boy, I'd hunt or fish,
play cowboy on my own with sticks for ridin high.
I'd a temper but cooled down real fast.

had some game roosters I got a holt of,
my sister Nell knew where but never told.

my brother Bud he loved me so
but he was young so hung on back when I
lit out for Dallas and the lights of town.

got myself a wife real fast,
fixed up a place with Margaret and lived a life.

me and some boys we got a car and was
on a tear, roamin the streets in search of booty,
we found too much attention from the Law
and I became a 'likely' at that time, they got
to know my name real well.

Margaret and me we had twin boys
but one died small and Margaret went away.
I never saw my son again.

I bought a pit bull, moved back home
but when my dog tore off little Marie's dress
Momma said we had to go.

I fell in love again, this time with Pearl
but when we had a baby girl things went downhill quick.

I was on my own with low-grade friends
but to my brother Bud it looked like glamour times.

from Denton down to Waco I got to stealin cars
and it was good until the Law caught me up
and locked me in.

that's when my kin they brought the wagon down for me:
got work and picked along to San Antone
to show the judge some good and proper ways.

my daddy's nails were ripped right off his hands
by prickly plants, Momma slept below the wagon.
they worked for vittles, silage for the horse and
that old judge, he said I could go free.

one day while walkin on the street
I met a preacher's daughter name of Blanche.
she called me *Daddy*, I called her *Baby*,
man, she was a looker, things was fine.

I told my youngest brother LC,
and I told him true,
you never break the law until you're caught.

hardscrabble sweet-mouthed girl

I was better than the rest from the minute I was born,
my daddy was a bricklayer in the midst of sodbusters.

I was the most beautiful of babies: eyes blue as Texas sky
and a mind could glean anythin: in Sunday School

when I was a toddler I sang my heart out for the crowd!
They wanted hymns, I tossed out "He's a Devil in His Own Home Town."

It rang right through those shaky old pews!
All I wanted was fame, to get away from the dreariness,

but Daddy died when I was small and Momma cried all day.
We lived in hell or Cement City and school was all I had:

won every prize for writin and for my speech and spellin,
loved a sweet-talk boy named Roy and married fore I turned 16.

We set up house two blocks from my own momma
but that was still too far and every night I cried.

Handsome Roy was just a thief. He left me for the road then
the jailhouse. I went to servin food and drink at Marco's, then

the other spot downtown right near the courthouse. Shoot,
those days were fine til hard times hit and all those cafes shut.

I wanted love, I wanted things like in the talkies, yearned
for big excitement, not much else to do but drink and dance

but one sweet night I headed for my brother Buster's house.
His party changed my life forever.

Clyde at Buster's party

Clarence brought me & I was lookin round when she walked in the air it-
self just turned to somethin new, blonde hair flyin firecracker eyes explorin
everythin & when she seen me, her face it just blossomed with clear inten-
tions, I couldn't let the chance pass: stretched out my hand, stood close,
brought her next the window so I could show her which was my fancy ride

talk goin on around us, her blue eyes steady, hair full of light streamin in
from the porch, after I kissed her she gave a little smile & crushed near flat
agin me when I held her, she no taller than a pony, thought I coulda picked
her up & run, heard she had a husband in the joint, she said it weren't
real, she was quick as a hiccup, bored in school, what to do in a hole like
Cement City when yer hurtin for more & nothin ever happens, never saw
another want the same so fierce

to drive & be alive the way we could if we had chances & the world ran
right

if Jesse James

writes letters to the press, then I do too, if he takes mad chances, you bet
I do, if he gives two bucks to a man so he might drink the health of Jesse
James, I will do the very same, I will, never mind the conductor dead,
never mind the shootin of the innocents, I done that too, I have felt the
same as he, if he moves outside the law with his brother, Buck & I will call
ourselves a gang, if the Pinkertons hurt his momma, this is the grievous
truth, the Law will do the same most anywhere, if he writes about that I
will too, if he takes the name of Mr. Howard, then that will be my name,
them bad times he had in Northfield, in Gallatin, or when he was an army
man & wild, I'd like to talk with him of courage & the ride

his momma sold the pebbles off his grave, maybe mine will do the same,
his killer was a coward, will mine be a coward too?

BABY THUGS CAPTURED

Barrow, the Youngest of the Trio, Makes Most Spectacular Attempt To Escape Capture

MIDDLETOWN, MARCH 21. —— AP ——
Three young desperadoes were finally ap-
prehended after a series of car thefts, armed
robberies and shootouts. The three, named as
William Turner, Emery Abernathy and Clyde
Barrow, are locked up in the Waco jail awaiting
trial on charges of burglary and bank robbery.

Living up to their recent nickname of the
Baby Dumbells, they botched an attempted
escape by driving right towards the officers.
Barrow tried to elude his captors by hiding out
beneath a house for several hours and stealing
another car before a desperate race down a
one-way street.

One unnamed officer of the court was over-
heard to say that all would likely serve their
time at Eastham Prison Farm.

The Waco Times-Herald, March 21, 1930

Clyde: Prison Farm

1. one-way wagon

weren't no wagon but a cage upon the long bed of a truck, chained by the neck we climbed aboard, from Waco all the way I wondered what I'd see when we arrived, I was a slinky kid & shook inside my bones for thinkin on it all

Ralph Fults told me of 'the bat,' the beatin as they laid men out upon the floor, sand laced into wounds, the screamin & the stench, he talked about the barrel how they'd make you ride all night & day, legs numb & hands bound tight, to keep our spirits up we talked of Jesse James & William Bonney, how they'd've had em on, those bastards, how they'd've had em on

the wagon kept on rollin, there was no goin home

2. punk

I just turned 20 when they sent me down to Eastham, Ed Crowder, six foot
tall & twice my weight, he was a robber & a runner afore he come inside
these walls & no one caused no trouble when he were boss con of our hell
hall, he said I was his bitch & laid his hands on me & ripped me from
behind, I felt myself tore down one push upon the next

I wanted to die but I will kill him first afore I go

Aubrey Scalley, doin 50 years, he took that murder on his head for me,
he was an honest man, there was some good men there, for true

3. cripple

when I come to Eastham, I had never truly felt the cruel beak of despair, Bonnie did not write me for too long but I reckoned this: she weren't made to be no nun

10 hours a day workin the woodpile, runnin back & forth from where we sleep & eat, high riders chasin down the slowpokes & I know I'll be one soon (they beat us down like rented mules, it is their fun)

I took the axe to my left foot chopped off my big toe, part of another, no damn good to man nor beast they let me free, I was a cripple all my days beyond

I got me one big plan: break right into Eastham, free some boys & take my sweet revenge for what the Law has done to me

CONVICT DIES IN
PEN FIGHT IN HOUSTON

Convicted Robber Is
Stabbed 15 Times In Brawl

HOUSTON, OCT. 30. —— AP ——
Ed Crowder, 30, convicted Houston bank
robber was killed late last night in a knife
fight with another convict in the barracks of
the Eastham State farm, according to reports
from Capt. B. B. Monzingo.

In a desperate battle that threw the bar-
racks into turmoil and sent several hundred
convicts scurrying for safety, Crowder met
death after suffering 15 stab wounds on his
chest, back and body.

The Dallas Morning News, October 30, 1931

Darlin

Why don't something happen? I wrote in my diary
until one night it did.

From the first second I saw him I knew he was the one: he wanted
all I wanted from a life, to claw our way to where we aimed to be.

He looked to me kinda like Ronald Colman with his fine clothes
and fancy car and when I stood up close he felt just right beside me.

He had thick dark wavy hair and dancin eyes,
said he'd sometimes felt too short with other girls.

My momma even said she liked the dimple that would pop out
when he smiled. I worshipped him, there was no doubt.

When he went down to Eastham I did alright to wait but
a year and some is long when you're yearnin.

Got myself a new man and a job but found no joy to life with
nothin goin on until I looked up from the couch and

saw him hobble in the door, my darlin wounded boy,
come for me at last. I leapt right in his arms!

Clyde and Ray and Ralph formed up the Barrow gang and I went too,
we were together now, let no one dare say otherwise.

nincompoop

I don't like it when they poke at me & call me dumb as dirt

one night a true blue norther & the roads were all awash, it turned out my baby Bonnie had to ride a mule, our luck had flown for cash or cars that time & on her painful ride she musta thought who is this knucklehead I left my momma for?

nothin much to eat & sleepin in our cars, smellin bad some days & Bonnie tryin to look her best, hair combed & makeup on, real smart she was & kindly

sometimes I'd hide beneath a house yet they always caught me, inferior machinery to blame I do insist that Fords are best I could not get my hands on one that day, what must she have thought the time I ran towards the Law & right on past, two of em reloadin. I got away, they put her in the slammer but she wrote a real good poem inside, that's all she says about it now, she loves me so

I was best when on the road, high ridin in some fine flathead v8 I stole, found money in em sometimes, mostly just for food & some shelter, clean white shirts & ammo for the road

I'm not a fancy man like Pretty Boy or Dillinger but I was feared of nothin when at the wheel, if they were here they'd like to say so, sure as shootin, never been so good upon my feet

MULE THEFT CHARGED
TO MAN AND WOMAN

KAUFMAN, TEX. —— UP —— Charges of 'mule theft,' auto theft and burglary were drawn here against a man giving his name as Jack Sherman, 27, Tulsa, Okla., and a bob-haired blonde woman giving her name as Betty Thornton, 23, Dallas.

Covered with mud, they were captured 25 miles southeast of here after a pursuit and gun battle in the best manner of the old west. Sherman was shot in the hand and a second man escaped in the battle.

The chase began when Police Chief David Drennan saw two men and a woman entering the Robert H. Brock store at Mabank. They fled west in a car believed stolen at Tyler. It mired after a few miles.

As Drennan and Officer Ballard approached the trio mounted two mules and splashed through the five miles north to Kemp. There a second automobile was stolen and turned southeast toward Mabank.

It too mired. The three continued their flight on foot and fired on the officers as they approached. The mud-spattered girl, weighing less than 100 pounds, said she had no part in the fight and "didn't know what she did during it." She carried no weapons.

The Dallas Times Herald, April 21, 1932

Bucher dead & Clyde's to blame

me, Ted Rogers & John Russell stole a car & went to check out a likely spot in Hillsboro, combo jewelers, general store, optician practice & garage, got to be a little somethin goin down there, but when I saw that woman starin at my mug I recollected how I knew her kid & said to call it off

but Ted & Johnny liked the place a lot & wouldn't hear it was jinxed like I knew it was

I sat outside smokin & when I heard a shot I waited for the worst: they got but 40 bucks, some bracelets in a bag & old man Bucher dead on the floor

I had not bin inside that night, I did not fire a shot & my mug was the only one she recalled

Stringtown

August 5th round 9 pm Ray, Ross & me drove into Stringtown, they'd
started up the dancin & the girls looked cute as possums, the band had
started "Way Down Yonder" & Ross right quick was up there dancin to
that tune

outa nowhere sheriff Maxwell put his foot up on the runnin board & I
could see his face as he blew back on the grass, six bullets deep inside him
yet he lived to tell

I did not drive too far afore the tire caught some damn culvert & the car
flipped sideways, so me & Ray we started runnin, there is no safety then,
they was close to us all shoutin & the gunfire flew like spray, I turned &
aimed direct & smooth & he fell dead, the undersheriff Moore

right then I reckoned it, no end of runnin til the end

WD Jones's tale

I seen Clyde Barrow first when I was five years old. We was all camped out beneath the Oak Cliff Viaduct in Dallas. Nowheres else to go.

My kin cept Momma and my brothers died of flu and that's when Momma grew tight to Cumie. They was true friends those two.

We all rode down together pickin cotton all the way with the aim to beg a judge to let Buck out of jail.

Me and LC best of buds those days. Grew up together doin what all we could, I did not read nor write. Would do anythin for money, stealin bikes and such and bigger things.

LC had his daddy's car one Christmas Eve and we'd bin dancin, drinkin brew. When LC's brother Clyde said he could use my help I reckoned that was swell. It seemed sorta big to be out there with them, Clyde and Bonnie famous. It was good to know they could count on me.

Within one day Clyde killed Doyle Johnson: shot him in the face in Temple, Texas and I had murder on my head. I'd lived but 16 years.

When they say Clyde Champion Barrow was the best, hell I knowed that cause I rode with him. He'd drive 1000 miles if he thought the Law was close.

No way they'd be caught alive, they knew their end. Nights I'd see him on his knees, I reckon prayin for his soul or for a longer life. Hell-bent on gettin round the Law but sometimes he'd get tired.

We used to wear each other's clothes. He was a small man just like me, quiet as a cat with dogs close. Never wanted dirt upon his skin. Never used bad language though he had a temper and he and Bonnie sure could fight.

Eight months I lasted til I'd had enough of blood and hell. Near Dexter, Iowa where Buck and Blanche were caught I took some buckshot to the face and chest and I was bleedin out, heck, all of us were hurt real bad. But Clyde, he done took some farmer's car and we three lit a shuck right outta town.

I left em when they'd healed enough they could get by without me. I hooked it back to Texas and got turned in to the Law. Did my time, married, found some happiness in life. That damn fool movie made it look so fine, like it was sorta glamorous, our ride, but it was hell.

long distance drive

Clyde knew all the routes from Texas up to Oklahoma,
Kansas, Iowa and back, on and on into the cloak of night,

evenin lights rushin past, meager dwellins in the fields,
a woman standin at the window, or in the golden distance, a child or

someone small. Some nights I'd waken, not remember where we'd
been or where we were headed, I'd say Sugar where d'you think we are?

He always knew which way to go, how fast to drive to get there.
Sleepless, I'd get goin on polishin and loadin the guns,

sometimes in my head thinkin up a rhyme or two, maybe I'd say them. I'd
be pleased to do the watchin when it was Clyde's turn to sleep,

listenin to the night and thinkin on our lives,
just lookin for the sun to rise.

Blanche's complaint

What was I to Clyde or Bonnie but a body
to buy their meals or wash their dirty clothes?
I never asked for more than to be up close to Buck,
who I would follow through the drippin
jaws of hell, and did, you tell me if I lie.

No sense denyin: Buck was a married man
with babies long before he saw my face but swore
it wasn't the same with me. And I'd been hurt
in marriage too: a man I never wanted
bought me from my momma.
I begged my daddy save me but he would not leave the farm.

It was not long before my body broke and I was left barren,
he used me way too bad. I left that man, I ran away.
No one ever cared for me at all but Buck.

I fell in love with Buck first thing, convinced him
to go back inside and do out his full time.
I missed him sore but then good times all on our own til
those two show up, real drunk: Buck's favourite Clyde,
and Bonnie, with their big talk of fame and pride.

I begged Buck not to go
but from March until July we rode together.

We played at cards, slept late
and sometimes were happy,
drove through 10 or 15 states.
I would not know the day nor hour,
shootin screamin, all the blood.
I prayed we'd die together
Buck and I.
No one heard that prayer.

Buck knows blood runs thick

when told I got full pardon I was happy as a gopher
in soft dirt. Blanche and me we went to see her momma on the farm
for what she'd been pinin for was her dog Snowball
and he'd been livin there. we made plans together for a life.

when Bud showed up with Bonnie and that kid they were full lit, I knowed
it but did not care, for Bud and me, well, kin is kin, and Bonnie
crawled in bed with Blanche while WD kept lookout from the sill.
there was rifles leanin up against the walls.

Blanche she begged me not to go but all we'd planned was holiday,
the five of us we'd have a time, and Bonnie wanted girl-talk after
all the drivin round with just them boys. I said ok, we're goin.
Blanche she made that Snowball ride along.

the Joplin place, chatter, laughin, tasty food and soft warm beds,
someone watchin out for us: the guard walkin round and round,
we paid him good — it was too good to last.
Blanche looked sweet as pie, she liked droppin puzzle
bits in place while we dealt out the cards and drank.

we had ourselves some fun til late one night the Law come.
I shot one stone dead, I blew another's limbs away.
to name them, they were Harryman, McGinnis and later
it was Marshall Humphrey, Lawmen all. them murders meant
the Chair, the spot where I was headed then, both me and Bud.
I did not care, liked it while it lasted, it was for kin that's all.

Blanche's first firefight: Joplin

I did not know how gunfire tears apart a body, saw a Lawman layin there with brains spilled down his shoulders and his arm bust off. To close my eyes it is seared there, blood dark and thick, soft grey folds of brain.

I was carryin WD to the car just draggin him, his chest and side bubblin with blood and Snowball lit out just never stopped runnin though I called and called.

The sound of bullets whizzin past my head, for a moment I thought I could outrun them and gather up those things I'd left behind, the camera and the papers and the clothes.

Screamed so hard inside the car because it was all gone, my hopes for life with Buck, my dreams, all dead, everything I'd held tight in my hands all pried away that day, the cards that Bonnie dealt me out.

like us: the photographs left behind at Joplin

we come shinin from the tray as real as fleshed-out fine-boned forms
even our shoes flashin, we are some fun jokers
are not coarse, cannot lie, do not limp or bleed
are kind & funny, desperately in love
we are you but better, no denyin

fix us there, that moment when you like us, want to be like us

we was never truly famous til now

nothing lies more than a photograph

Pearly teeth and a cigar: I never smoked it.
Finger on a trigger, did not fire a gun at all.

Knew how to clean it well, lightnin happy,
sharp clothes, tiny teeth smiling,

lips like hairline fractures.
Moll disguised as moll.

Sunday clothes

a man gives a teachin to the world when he dress right, clean & well-kept,
soft hat tipped smooth: how a man should look all week if he wants to
know respect, get me some of that when I break into Eastham

starved by boll weevils then the Bog is not the route I chose: it is a soul's
death

I am a crippled thin short man but I dress well & when I roar past your
joint in Henry Ford's best machine you'll all come out to see me & you'll
cheer

Tulsa Okla
10th April.

Mr. Henry Ford
Detroit Mich.

Dear Sir: –
  While I still have got breath in my lungs I will tell you
what a dandy car you make. I have drove Fords exclusively
when I could get away with one. For sustained speed and
freedom from trouble the Ford has got ever other car skinned,
and even if my business hasent been strickly legal it don't hurt
eny thing to tell you what a fine car you got in the v8 –
            Yours truly
            Clyde Champion Barrow

prayer (Bonnie)

My momma raised me just this way:
each night to say my prayers and clean my heart out.

All I felt for Clyde made true for me again when
I woke up one night and saw him kneelin on the floor

just talkin to his Lord like I do. He looks so like a child
when down upon on his knees, the Lord must love him

as he does all little things. Look out for us, please, Lord
as surely no one else can. It feels like standin naked in the wind

each day to leave these cabins or the car and woods behind.
Sometimes in the dark my fears rise up and chase me.

Could come any time our final battle, and when it does I know my heart
will rest with you. I pray it will. I hope there will be rest. Amen.

the clothes that Blanche ran with

Golden yellow spring outfit with white detailin, white gloves and pumps to match (ruined by grease that time I drove the car). Gray silk flounced skirt modified cape shoulders and cloche hat, shoes with bows across the ankle. Light blue dress tiny buttons all up and down the front, deep scooped neckline. Multicolor cotton skirt, layers, short sleeved top tiny leather belt showin off my waistline. Blue crepe evenin gown with low-cut back and lace shoulders I hemmed up short to wear around the Joplin place. Tight yellow jodhpurs made me look so nice and trim and went real well with ridin boots (what I wore when we were caught).

end of day / Texas wind

I was not raised up to be genteel nor feeble yet the cruel heat that blows
across my face is like to wear me out, I drive into the pinewoods, settle in
the shade, shadows flow across my back like waves upon the Galveston
sand

when dust flies up like this we lean agin the boards & eat our meager meal
then settle in for all the needs of darkness, whoever has the turn to wake
& watch will spend the hours pickin grit from grim & anxious teeth

is this the glamour they describe when they write about our run? I feel the
shadows coil right round me, press my dog-tired head agin the ground

barrel fires

the flames reflect faces on our drive seein two good-lookers on a holiday,
rode up to Bay City, along the lakes, all over Chicago, why the hell not?
we're young

got a pass to see the World's Fair, girls wrapped up in ice cubes, midgets,
General Balbo & his 24 seaplanes all the way from Rome, fan dancers, sky
ride, we ate lyin on a beach most all the time

motor courts, long & dreamless sleeps, we did not listen to the news or
much outside, we laughed like hell, I sang some, Bonnie rhymed

I grieve that my old ma & pa have never felt as free

the day Fatty Arbuckle died

we hide in the woods & listen to the chatter, all the eyes of Texas lookin out for us, it is June '33 & the heat truly on, more than 100 in the shade for weeks now

a fat man like that, he'd surely tumble to the downs, we could have spoke together easy for he knew how falsehood feels

do they look down from Heaven & see us, all our dead ones? is there happiness at last?

the press said it was them that made us but it was our photos & her poems & our clothes, all the press ever done was deal a pack of lies

great big blue-eyed baby: Fatty Arbuckle, he knew the truth can crack your heart

the accident at Wellington

headin to meet up with Buck & I was drivin good then what the

off the road & in the air, comin down in silence, slow shift of bodies, foul-mouthed acrobats we are holy speckled flash & spark, clipped & turnin, headlights sizzlin on through air

the stock-still world

me & WD, we're standin there outside, shaky ringin head I turn to look, clipped blood bits flash, edge of river broken bridge

Bonnie pressed agin the engine locked there under the battery leakin thigh to ankle, bloody all the way to bone

TWO TEXAS DESPERADOES
KIDNAP TWO OFFICERS

Woman Companion Injured as
Car is Wrecked — Farm Family
Terrorized, One is Shot

WELLINGTON, TEXAS. JUNE 21 —— AP
Two machine-gunning motorists today terri-
fied a farm family, kidnapped two officers and
escaped with an injured woman companion
after their automobile plunged over a road
embankment.

Sherriff Dick Corey and City Marshall
Paul Hardy, kidnapped in the Sherriff's motor
car, were driven to near Erick, Okla., and left
wired to a tree. They identified the gunmen as
Clyde Barrow, Dallas (Texas) desperado and
Icy Barrow, his brother.

The New York Times, June 21, 1933

proud flesh

It was not bullets flyin round the risks we took
that carved my deepest scar, it was the drivin:

one mad night when Clyde flipped off the road
and all was sudden mayhem, overturn disaster,

knee to ankle burned into a flesh-made trench.
I do not now recall much of those early hours.

To wake and feel myself pried from the car
onto the legs of strangers, then into dark again

and drivin through the night, some woods-deep hidden room,
lifted into bed, from there to toilet when I needed it,

me screamin, drinkin brew, they poured all that they had
into my care and brought my sister there for aid and comfort.

Sobbed tears, prayed hard, pain greater than I could ever reckon.
I don't recall much til my leg drew up beneath me

and the evenins mornins afternoons all one long hurt and drink
like armor on the outside of an open wound, raised up and thick,

a bindin that held us fast. It was one thing Clyde did wrong
that wretched rushin night and crash there at the bridge,

but when alone, our wounds displayed one to the other, it was
a pledge of all we were, which would not break nor bend.

let's take em, Clyde said, and some people
thought he meant gunplay

there was the mail carrier Owens who rode with me & Ralph Fults outside
Electra, Texas, we took his car, he was scared bad & worse later when we
bust a chain blockin the Red River bridge to Oklahoma, there was gunfire
too but no one come to harm

later we pulled over, let him go, he was standin on the road next to his car,
come to askin what we planned on doin with it further up the road, we
said he'd get it back after a time, he said if it's all the same to us, he'd pre-
ciate if we burn it cause the government would likely have an obligation to
buy a new one for his use, I like that fella, he had some nerve

*

who lives in a town by the name of Hico? one warm afternoon with six
inside the car: Buck, Blanche, me & Bonnie & two strangers from there-
abouts, Mr. Darby & Miss Stone, they got some trouble on account of us,
bein chased & such, so we just took em in, I got steamed that day, WD
plain lost somewheres & our plan to hit a bank all gone to hell. Buck tellin
me shoot em but Bonnie started up that chat she liked so much & found
out what they done for a livin, Miss Stone was what they call a home dem-
onstration agent & man we laughed like hell about that, her all up in the
front with BAR clips fallin on her lap from where they shoulda stayed put,
but then Darby spoke up to say he was a practicin mortician, & Bonnie
made him promise to embalm us, she thought he would like that, we all
had a laugh about it, then we crossed the border into south Arkansas

*

right after the crash at Wellington WD & me we ran into laws Corey and
Hardy & took their car right quick with every gun we had just pointed at
their heads & I laid Bonnie on em as they sat in back, she had most ter-
rible great pain & I was drivin like the dogs was after me, I needed to get
back with Blanche & Buck real quick, I was riled up, real tense. so thought
I'd string those boys along a bit, asked if they'd heard tell of the Barrow

44

brothers, Hardy said he knew of Buck but no one by the name of Clyde, thought he had me there, when we caught up with the others they was sleepin in their car, Buck asked was I aimin to bump these two boys off & I said I done drove with em so long I got to likin em, we tied em to a tree & got away, they'd been real good to Bonnie

when we drive this way

When we drive this way I like to watch the blur of trees
in the dusty day, how they turn to blue at a certain hour

and I brush my hand across the cotton skirt to feel my hips
rise up against my fingertips. We drive so long and fast I forget

I wear my bones some days. When we stop in the cool of the shade,
bumpin through low brush and hidden, Clyde takes out the blanket

and spreads it out atop the dry grass, wild carrot lazy in the air on
either side and the low sun romance makes me pull my hair down

smooth across my cheeks, plump up my beret. He opens up the door to
me, the brown of his eyes so dark, his fine hand slips behind my back and

one beneath my knees so slow the pain still there and sometimes very bad.
Then I'm up and tuck my head to move on out into the hot still air,

hopin for some breeze. We lie on the blanket, eat some beans and find
some scraps of meat, share it out with care there is so little now

and sure I know I am not the pretty thing I used to be, I say how long will
you love me lookin like this. He says I am a liar but he is always sweet

that way, I do love him so. When will we die? Will it be together right
away or will there be some long slow time of grief.

talkin Spanish with the women
(Buck imagines William Bonney)

before I found my own ways,
I practiced what I heard the Kid would do:
used manners, looked them in the eyes,
whispered serious words.

I fell in love most eagerly
and married three times,
their soft mouths
shinin hair.

I never took the time for readin nor writin
the way the Kid could.
I reckon him a knowledgeable man,
knew how to parlay language of the south.

when Billy died, they say
many Spanish women mourned.

Blanche thinks on the night in Platte City

We were bone tired of it, sittin in our cabin at the tourist lodge, Buck polishin my ridin boots and sayin he reckoned we could move to Canada, live there without trouble. He'd always liked to hunt and trap and we could make a life there, leave the others long behind.

I walked on over to the store for soap and saw some folks just lookin at me strange and stopped their talkin when I passed among them. I found a weigh scale showed I'd lost near 20 pounds since startin on this run.

I went straight to Clyde's cabin to say things feel wrong but Clyde sent WD for sandwiches and beer and nothin further happened.

Later on we went to sleep then heard the Law move round outside and one shot another by mistake and that's when we started for the car, Bonnie hobblin there and Clyde full ready at the wheel, but WD and Buck and me we had to run some distance from where we were to the Ford,

bullets round us everywhere, some tore right into Buck, his arms and chest and took out some skull. I saw the brain clear open there, o my dear Daddy.

I dragged him to the car, Lord knows how, WD firin away above my head, time stretched out forever, nightmare flash.

I was leanin over Buck inside the car. I did not want him hurt no more but bullets smashed the glass and splinters ripped my eyes, I was near blind,

blood sloshin on the floor, Buck called out for water, told me he was hurtin just a little, Clyde drove on til he could see the sun.

BLOOD-STAINED DRESS FOUND NEAR SCENE OF GUN BATTLE

KANSAS CITY, JULY 22. —— AP ——
A woman's dress, described by D. R. Clevenger,
Platte county prosecutor, as being so blood-
stained that "it was impossible to tell the color
of the garment" was found in a pasture near a
tourist camp at Platte City. The camp was the
scene of a gun battle between peace officers and
two gunmen early Thursday. Officers believed
they wounded one of the men and also one of
the two women accompanying them. The Kan-
sas City office of the U.S. Bureau of Investiga-
tion say the men have been identified as Clyde
and Marvin (Buck) Barrow, sought for killings
in Joplin, Mo. and Alma, Ark.

Kansas City Star, July 22, 1933

WD: Dexfield Park

We pulled into a bunch of trees not far off from a river, figured it the place for Buck to die.

Clyde and I, we dug a grave but Buck lived on through that long night and days beyond. Clyde and Bonnie rode off for supplies while I told Buck and Blanche I'd had enough of outlaw life for good and they reckoned that was right.

I was 17 and needed to get home, get back to my momma.

Clyde brought back a lot of food and bandages, new clothes and a brand new Ford v8 sedan.

Someone was around just huntin blackberries I reckon, but saw us real clear. We was all layin on some blankets lookin poorly.

Not a likely gang.

At night we tried to sleep as best we could, Blanche in the car and Bonnie tendin Buck, two of the worst off types you could imagine. Clyde and me upon the ground.

A screech owl sailed above our heads, just hollerin.

When the posse came upon us, I knowed hell on earth.

Clyde's arm was shot up bad and half the way downhill Buck fainted.

It was over, I knew it then.

Bonnie in her nightgown draggin through the woods, Blanche screamin far behind us as the bullets kept on comin, dogs just barkin like mad, the darkness.

Stumblin on and on into the night, Clyde knew where he was headed and he found a farm, whistled hard for me to carry Bonnie. He had an empty .45 but when he waved it at the farmer that old coot was scared. He'd heard the Barrow gang were on the loose. He had no money for gas he said but we was welcome to his car.

We found some cans of kerosene, got away as far as green Nebraska.

Bonnie, awake in Dexfield Park

I swear I heard the lions callin though I know for sure
the zoo's been gone for years. It was as clear as daylight

with the moon high-strung. Stars so still I tried
to stir the waters of the sky with just my fingertip.

To lean down over Buck and see inside his brain
choked me hard. All else asleep, my job to watch.

I did not mind it. Hours passed swift as a dream.
The only thing I'd ever tell was this:

the screech owl sailin by?
I thought it was Buck's spirit runnin free.

Blanche recalls the capture

The dew was comin down and Buck was sleepin. We were pressed close up against a log, it was so cold and wet and someone shouted there they are, and right then it seemed like 30 men shootin at us with rifles. Buck come to again and took the pistol, I don't know if he even fired a shot before they hit him six more times. He threw his body over mine and held me in his arms, Baby he said, they got me this time and I believed the life was drainin from his body. I just went mad, I was screamin, beggin them to stop but then he breathed again and I fell on him cryin, I don't want you to die not here in this field, Daddy, I could not bear it, my Daddy needs white sheets to die on, but I kissed him goodbye. They took us God knows where and they were rough to him, though I begged them to be gentle and I lit his cigarette and asked for water for him. Was he angry at me that I gave up, I only wanted him to die in a bed and not be tore to shreds. They laid him out upon the floor, me cryin out as they led me through the door, screamin Goodbye Daddy, Goodbye

the doctor to Buck

Where are you wanted by the law?

wherever I bin I said.

the stench from my hurt head
keeps em all far across the room from me.
unless to give the needle
then they come close.

sometimes the needle makes me sleep
sometimes it makes me
talk then Momma and LC come
and there is weepin.

took Blanche away long time ago.
is this her with me now?
I grip the hand of a sweet girl:
please, please, don't go.

MRS. BARROW HELD AT PLATTE CITY

KANSAS CITY, JULY 26, —— AP —— Mrs. Blanche Barrow, 22-year-old wife of Marvin Ivan (Buck) Barrow, Dallas, Tex., gunman, arrived in Platte City early today from Iowa, where she and her husband were captured in a fight with officers near Dexter.

D.R. Clevenger, country prosecutor at Platte City, said Mrs. Barrow probably would be arraigned late today on a charge of assault with intent to kill in connection with the wounding of three men in a battle with officers at a tourist camp near Platte City.

Meanwhile her husband is in a dangerous condition in Perry, Ia., from wounds suffered in the battle at Dexter.

Kansas City Star, July 26, 1933

prayer (Clyde)

pray to find the way to Heaven, seems every day I get up & drive & drive
some more, weary of this life, here I am in this old motor court & near me
the woman I have loved most in this world, she is so dear to me that I ask
my woeful self what brought her to me, Lord, I must not be so bad as all
they think, here I am, okay with whatever is to come, you know that Lord
as I talk to you most nights like this, upon my knees

is it what I must expect, to go to Hell? is that where Buck is at? I do not
know if he knows your Ways, I always believed, all those pictures of you
& listened to those stories of your Pain, I don't know how you beared it
some bad times, why you didn't up & walk away but took the bad upon
yourself to save our wretched souls, you love us they say & it gives me peace
to know it as I lay down my head each night & let the dreams come on

the Eastham break: Clyde

bin dreamin of this for what felt like all my life, as if there was a clear
before, when I stood upright & felt complete & *after* was all the rest of it,
this kind of break was not what I was waitin for, I was the driver, only that

so many piled inside the car, two in the trunk & screamin all the way,
sweat & tales of jangled times behind: high riders bleedin from the mouth,
one fat white stomach punctured with sure aim, did not succumb for three
long days, pained & moanin, Law pressin close besides, *They gave me not
a dog's chance* what he whispered at the end

I was the driver: light up the Chair for me

to hide the guns was danger beyond all, to work with only one escape road
leads to hell, said at first I would not do the job this way but Bonnie said
I'd waited far too long, I went along, I was the driver

turned out some was caught & some pled out for deals, one boy who rode
away with us was Henry Methvin, he was goin down real fast those days,
the brains was Raymond Hamilton who started hangin round with scum, I
dropped him off, I knew he hated me, I broke him out

Law bosses called in Hamer, said it was my plan

CLYDE BARROW RESCUES FIVE CONVICTS
IN MACHINE GUN RAID ON PRISON FARM

2 GUARDS SHOT
AS LEAD HAILS
FROM SIX GUNS

The Paris Evening News, January 17, 1934

Hamer in repose

It was the raid on Eastham prison farm —
Hamilton and Methvin runnin loose
and Barrow at the wheel —
I was called in —

I learned their ways —
the car they drove, I drove —
I carried the same guns
and would have worn their clothes
had I been puny like them —

All I care for's doin work that's fair,
not carin what I'm paid —
that's how I live and why
I'm unsurpassed —

Some hate me for my honest tongue —
I turn from them

CONVICT CAUGHT
IN TEXAS.

HUNTSVILLE, TEXAS. JAN 17. —— AP
J. B. French, one of the five convicts who escaped
when Clyde Barrow, Texas desperado, raided
the Eastham State prison farm yesterday, has
been recaptured. Bloodhounds chased French
into the cabin of Gabe Wright, a Negro living
near the prison farm. Wright pointed his shot-
gun at the convict and held him until the farm
dog sergeant and his posse arrived.

The New York Times, January 18, 1934

I love the car

because within its scope there is both gratitude and anguish.
It has saved my life and stolen my ability to run.

It has let us ride together, knee to knee
and thighs pressed close beneath the pig-blood dash,

world flyin by and we could let it go.
Because deep within the soft back seat the revolver

smiles and winks, ammunition calls out to be housed,
rifles lurk. Forget about the typewriter, all its keys and promise.

There is no end to work that can be done. Because we rolled along
with eight after the Eastham break and we were soarin then,

the car could've run on nerves and fear alone, four thin tires bouncin on
the rutted earth, yet freedom's what we knew that day,

all Clyde had promised and he never broke his word.
Because it took us on a holiday or two, cruised us past some likely marks,

left every other damn car chokin in its dust, offered up
a welcome bed where drunk or sober bones could rest, a carpet floor

both merciful and thirsty, a space where we felt safe enough to sleep.
It made us look like winners in this life.

Easter Sunday

Some days it was the love of strangers held me up
when I might tumble in pain and need for kin,

the hunger of our worn out lives. They thought me
buoyed by freedom, wild abandon, loved my glamour.

Easter Sunday changed it all, and quick. Then I was
the nasty dirty moll who shot Lawmen dead, like

that rookie Murphy, his first day on the job.
They said I shot and shot him as he laid on the ground.

They said I laughed. They said it was me the cause
of much loud weepin at the church when his fiancée Tullis

walked her bridal gown right down the funeral aisle.
But I never glimpsed his face. Drunk Henry's the one who done it.

Henry Methvin stole our fame. He shot away
all the love they bore us, the end of our good name.

TWO STATE HIGHWAY PATROL OFFICERS SLAIN AS THEY APPROACH AUTO CLOSE TO GRAPEVINE

BARROW AND RED-HEADED WOMAN BELIEVED TO HAVE SHOT DOWN POLICEMEN

Desperado and Cigar-Smoking Bonnie Parker
Thought to Have Been Waiting for Arrival

Fort Worth Star-Telegram, April 2, 1934

heat

1. Bonnie

I been sweatin in the Texas dirt for all my life, swaggered off to school
then piled plates and saucers in the steamin sink at work

and flirted with the customers. Could once tell the time of a hot day
by how the sun cracked in beneath the blinds.

We drag a faded dusty tunnel in ruts behind the car,
I wish it were my shroud.

2. Clyde

once I'd gottem in the Ford the only thing inside my head's the sound of
my own heart, a goddamn drum, shoes off, guns pressed upside my legs I
drove, the screamin goin on behind & blood sloshed upon the floor

I did not know if it was mine or theirs nor did I care right then

that was heat, no time for thinkin

3. Frank Hamer, Texas Ranger

Sure, I've seen their kind before —
just kids without a right thought
in their heads —

but once Clyde killed Gene Moore
a deputy in Stringtown, Oklahoma —
he'd know it was the Chair for him —

and Malcolm Davis,
Wes Harryman and more —
lawmen plain —

and after that last breakout
I knew I'd hunt them down
like a blue tick on a black bear —
and I'm no liar

And the like of us may never hope
For death to set us free
For the living are always after you
And the dead are after me

— Bonnie Parker, from "Outlaws"

In the early morning of May 23, 1934 a six-man posse (including Prentiss Oakley, who fired the first shot, and Frank Hamer, who fired the last) lay in the woods listening for the approach of Bonnie and Clyde. Henry Methvin's father Ivy parked his truck on the side of the road as a decoy. Buddy Goldston was driving his logging truck toward them all.

1.

36 hours we bin in this brush
just waitin

Seems like these insects roar

I've sweated through my clothes
and to the earth beneath

but I believe Frank Hamer is as good
as he seems to be

2.

I could hear them comin
quite a while ago
but kept my counsel —

best in these pure moments
not to brag —

3.

am I an evil man?
they promised me a pardon for my boy

to sell a body out
is damn familiar

not an evil man
not like them
but like all things biblical
like walkin through a nightmare of our own

4.

love this land, could find a place & settle here, bring Momma & all who
look for peace, just drivin this way leads to thinkin clear & clean
the bushes sing with praise

5.

Hot wind takes away my appetite for life. My red tam
lyin in the back, I press my ruby shoulders down.

Though I am now one ugly scrawny girl
I can still look right and dress real sharp.

6.

he better be the best
for I hear them comin

I believe we're gonna be
famous this day
shoot the souls right outta them

7.

Louisiana, sure a fine life, don't you be no lie

8.

hell
don't they know a man
has got to work on this road?
I got some riders
up here in the cab with me
and we all see the same

a fancy car
an old green truck broke down
some fella runnin away

9.

heart beatin so hard
I can barely hold the rifle steady
blood poundin in my head
in my fingertips

10.

what's that Ivy doin? I bought that truck for him & know it inside out
he seen my face but then he turned & run from me

11.

I can see his whole head clear as day
within my sights
small man
fine and jaunty hat

12.

Waxy paper in my hand, sick of fried bologna
but my thin bones require a feedin every day.

Look at Ivy hop away like that, hands on his belly.
I cannot run to save my life no more.

13.

I do believe I am the righteous
the righteous hand of Law —
and will exercise my obligations
here and now —

without one shot fired
enfold them —

wait for what's to come right now
call for their surrender —

14.

fixin to slow right over & help him change the tire, why's he runnin from
me now?

15.

just one pull
upon this trigger

16.

Ivy runnin then I turn to Clyde
and see his hat fly off, it is the moment.

All the angels comin for me
now

17.

one long high scream
from her then
we are all firin
then runnin toward them there

18.

what is this before me?
a battleground of fire
upon one car

19.

get down into the dirt
can I get further down
a hail of fire
hell of fire
rains upon them

20.

I look down into the car
and point my gun
and I shoot and shoot again
until I'm done —

when I turn
I cannot hear them —
the men who did not follow my command —

21.

I pull the truck up next to them
and look down upon their bodies leakin blood
glass and metal everywhere

I wish I had not been upon this road
this day

22.

we are deaf to one another
gunfire smoke just hangin in the air

is this some anger dream
of what my life is like?

a borrowed gun to kill them with
and with my first shot fired
I did

23.

Her lip hung nearly off her face
her whole dress soaked with gore —
and still I shot and shot her more —

24.

can I stand up?
where can I go to now to get away from here?

they better keep their word
I did, I did it

SHOOTING DESCRIBED

"We Just Shot the Devil Out of Them," Officer Says

ST. LOUIS, MAY 23. —— AP —— "We just shot the devil out of them."

Thus Frank Hamer, former Texas ranger captain, today described in a copyrighted telephone interview with the St. Louis Post-Dispatch the slaying near Arcadia, La. of Clyde Barrow and Bonnie Parker.

"Sure," he said, "I can tell you what happened this morning. We just shot the devil out of them, that's all. That's all there was to it. We just laid a trap for them, a steel trap, you know, Bessemer steel, like gun barrels are made of."

St. Louis Post-Dispatch, May 23, 1934

Hamer whispers

Lone wolf by nature, I gathered up a crew
who wouldn't listen —
I did know what was comin —
I can hear ahead of most —
see bullets in mid air
and there were many on that day —

It was like passin through a dream world —
deaf and walkin in cordite clouds —
could smell that sweet and unreal scent of blood
mixed with her light perfume —

I'd be a legend now —
but not like them —
they'll be the famous ones,
I'll not say one more word

death car

With gore and glass and the reek it is towed to town,
the wrecker breaking down before a schoolyard,
children all running out to view the dead
within: Bonnie's lip near severed from her mouth,
Clyde with head blown open,
hum of heat and insects thick as thieves.

It comes to rest in the town of Arcadia, home to 1000 souls
and a herd of 16,000 try to get an up close view:
one man tries to harvest Clyde's pretty ear, another his trigger finger,
bits of Bonnie's hair and dress are snipped away,
Clyde's body is a smear of red, wet rags.
Bonnie has hearts tattooed upon her thigh, beer sells
for two bits and you can't get a thin ham sandwich at any price.

There are 17 entry wounds in Clyde, 26 in Bonnie.
They are photographed frail and naked on gurneys,
sent to separate funeral homes.
Someone offers Henry 10 grand for his son's body
and Emma Parker can no longer hide her hatred for Clyde.

Meanwhile the Ford v8 flathead sits in the Arcadia impound lot
pocked by 167 bullets, filthy, but with engine still running smooth
as silk. The posse say it belongs to them, sweet ambush booty
along with all the guns and cash and trinkets from the ride.

Ruth Warren disagrees: that damn car she says was stolen April 29
from her place in Topeka, Kansas. She comes to drive it home,
then rents it out to Charles W. Stanley who loads it
on a flatbed and tours it round the land for free,
though a dime per person donation would help towards expenses.

Cumie Barrow and Emma Parker join the car on tour
in March of '35, a paycheck is a paycheck after all.
Henry has a job to talk about his boys and Marie handles tickets
for the show entitled Crime Does Not Pay,
not long before they head back home to Dallas.

Stanley runs the Death Car Tour well into the 40s.
People fall upon their knees and weep to see it.
Arguments break out and lawyers make their fees.

The car moved hand to hand from state to state
and rests today upon the floor in
Whiskey Pete's Casino, Primm, Nevada,

the car they lived and died in like a shrine:
damn you Henry Ford, you and your knack for slick design.

carried in the car

1. Remington Model 8, Remington Model 11 sawed off, Remington Whippet, model 1887, 10 gauge riot gun, 10 gauge semi-automatic shot gun, 10 gauge Winchester lever-action, BAR custom made scattergun, up to nine Colt automatic pistols, BAR twenty-shot magazines, thousands of rounds of ammunition

2. Remington portable typewriter

3. drafts of poems, handwritten as well as typed by Bonnie

4. two women's purses (including a marriage license, title of 1929 Marmon purchased from Carl Beaty, divorce papers, criminal pardon issued to Buck by governor Miriam Ferguson, compact, combs, tubes of lipstick)

5. suitcases of clothing, earrings, wigs, hair dye and jewelry

6. a six string wood guitar

7. a saxophone

8. a medical kit with salve and bandages

9. cigarettes and matches

10. liquor and some flasks

11. cash

12. sandwich wrappers and odds and ends from meals

13. a dog named Snowball until the night in Joplin

14. a rabbit named Sonny Boy for several weeks after Easter, 1934

15. stained, torn or worn out clothing

16. a camera, rolls of film

17. 15 sets of stolen license plates

18. hats

19. random issues of magazines: *The Master Detective, True Detective, True Crime*

20. sewing implements

21. newspapers

22. Clyde's shoes lay on the floor beside him, he drove barefoot

23. one, two, three, four, five, six, seven or eight people at any one time

24. decks of cards

25. jigsaw puzzles

26. blankets

27. lemons to freshen the breath after drinking

28. a makeup case

29. Rand McNally road maps

200 yellow roses
(LC Barrow recollects his brother's funeral)

out of a low flyin plane
petals onto Clyde's shared grave

an outburst of my tears
I tried to hold up Momma but
we could neither of us stand

out of the blue Texas sky
some gambler threw his chips
into the open grave

dark jackets hangin off the bones
of those who press up close

heard there's a bigger spellbound crowd
across town for Bonnie
but no roses seen fallin there

if faith could raise them
they could hijack that gambler's
rented plane

getaway arrow through the weepin day

BARROW IS BURIED; THOUSANDS VIEW BODY

Private Funeral Tomorrow is Planned for Bonnie Parker by Her Mother.

DALLAS, TEXAS. MAY 25 —— AP —— Clyde Barrow, until three days ago the most feared killer in the south-west — was buried at sunset tonight on a chalky west Dallas hillside near his boyhood home.

Souvenir hunters snatched roses, gladioli and peonies from the mound of earth as Barrow's mother was led wailing away.

Thousands of persons had viewed his body.

Far across the city in a funeral parlor, the shot-torn body of Clyde's gun-woman, Bonnie Parker, was ready for transfer to the home of her mother, Mrs. Emma Parker, awaiting private funeral services Sunday.

The Dallas Journal, May 25, 1934

Blanche remembers the long ride

I used to believe in love the way believers play their faith,
close to the chest, fannin it out when they need it most.
I could've used some back there when my mother sold me
for a song. A hard-handed man he broke me surely,
no more hopes for children or a tender word at best.
My daddy was a kind man but so poor he could not cope
with anythin but slow tillin of the dry soil
sun-up, sun-down, wind that brought the farm indoors.
The only thing saved him was his deathlike sleep, yet
dreams, dreams go on.

Never expected to find what love was really like,
how it pulled me to Buck like a chigger to the hairline,
his warm brown eyes, his hands that mastered anythin
he put his mind to. We had such plans for livin, he and I.
In some woodland bright safe place far away from all
we'd known before, we would be fine and free, we said so
all the nights in tourist camps lyin awake
listenin to passin cars, then the storm of bullets and
blood that burst in streams on the floor
out of the dead upon their backs.

Who could ever have reckoned how bad it would become,
the nights I'd sit up on the car and watch the stars,
taste of terror in my throat and gore on my thin hands.
Some nights I could not see the moon for all the horror in the way.
Or maybe it was hunger or the endless sleepless days
when all we had was fame not the kind I ever wanted:
outlaw woman. They didn't even know my real name.
I would have gone most anywhere with Buck but
they would not let me be there at the end, both of us broken,
no use any more.

When we first met on that road in sad West Dallas
he was the most beautiful man I'd ever seen, and he loved me so.
Even my daddy liked him: he was good all the way down to the bone.
Went to serve out his whole term because I asked.
I wish he'd stayed there now, or maybe gone to school
or left his kin behind. It was all on goddamn Clyde
what happened, we were doomed, I knew it from the start.
There was so much to hope for in those dusty early days,
his arms around me, all the future still to come.

Marie

me and LC were born the last of all us kids

in 1931 we hitched the shack upon a wagon bed, hauled it
down to Eagle Ford, a dusty road and middle of The Bog,
me inside it all the time, just ridin

my daddy built the roof above our heads, first one on the campground,
and a two-holer out back so all we knew were plumb
jealous of our ways

learned just what I could from my big bros, like
how to spur a rooster for a fight, real good I was
but not so good as Buck

one year for Christmas Bud gave me the gift I craved: a bicycle,
sure it were stole, I rode it like a wildcat,
a bike is hard in ruts but I could fly

late night on the road
I'd watch my brothers and their girls drive by
they was most famous then,
not long before they died

LC and me, we got to fightin Baldy Whatley,
he shot into the shack into Momma's face
so she was mostly blind

I was not at her funeral, did not see her to the grave,
I was too busy in the Walls, doin my time

can I ever let it go,
this shame and grievin?

me and LC, we did love Bud,
LC mourned him all his life and ofttimes
when he spoke of him he cried

half: Henry Methvin

Half grown when I went up to Eastham,
half my life already spent

18, a roughneck on the plains
when some punk laid old hands on me
I cut his throat and took his car
but ended up inside and that punk lived
to tell the Law I was just a liar

Eastham's where Clyde Barrow was,
his time there was the worst,
the brutal ways, the weariness, the nights:
he chopped his foot to get release
but said he'd come and break me out one day

My folks, they near went mad to get me free,
but weeks before my time was up
Clyde sprung me like he said,
Clyde Barrow always kept his word

I brought them once or twice to Bienville Parish
where life was real lush, thick forests
and mossy shade,
a house for them, a bed for sleepin,
my people round to talk and share a jar

Clyde kept sayin they were near the end
and it was plain that Bonnie drank most all the time
to dull the pain, the homesickness, the fear

I soon got to worryin,
it was not the end I hoped for
nor my mom nor pop
who said the pair were bad

Alone one day I said to Ma
there could maybe be a deal
to let me off the charges, sure
there had to be some plan

But Easter Sunday, in the buzzin Texas heat
I leaned against the car
and watched while Clyde and Bonnie slept,
they'd planned a picnic with their folks
and Bonnie shared her flask,
I wasn't thinkin clear
I raised my BAR and shot two Lawmen
off their bikes upon the road,
then laid more lead into them down there,
both blown to hell and gone

Not half the papers told the truth,
most wrote it was Bonnie
shot them as they bled upon the ground,
their heads bounced up and down
like rubber balls

but hell, I knew full well what I had done
while she lay drunk inside the car,
Sonny Boy the rabbit hugged up in her arms

and it was the Chair for sure
so my pa Ivy done the deal:
stood helpless by his broke-down truck
that mornin, May of '34,
he slowed them down and then he ran

Lawmen lie like no others,
they sent me back to jail,
Pa died one night of those long years,
crashin up some car

One night in '48 not long into my freedom
I drank some brew and took to wanderin the tracks,
curled myself up nestlike for a sleep,
too drunk and spent to hear the post-Depression,
post-War boomin engine bearin down,
that SP locomotive cut me clean in half

```
cause: shotgun
(William Daniel "WD" "Dub" "Deacon" Jones,
May 12, 1916 - August 20, 1974)
```

Ever look a 12-gauge in the eye?

I done that, cause that's what done me, three blasts sent me to the next
world, my chest filled with lead, my head with memory.

The best and worst of days back then.

I cannot lose the noise of that old ride though I done my time for sure and
worked all my years thereafter.

I was mean when drunk but mostly kindly, and sweet on some good
women.

I lived next door to Momma like any righteous son.

It was a woman ended me. All I had need of was a place to crash.
She called out to her boyfriend who I was. He'd read my talk in *Playboy*
and knew my past. He jumped right up and shot me dead on the front
porch. I was a famous man in pieces on the ground and the boyfriend
proud as hell to have my blood on his hands.

camera eye

Look in the mirror and look in the mirror and think of the times
I thought myself beautiful, all the looks that came my way

from strangers, clothin that feels more like tatters than fresh
laundered crepe, for a bed to sleep in, a proper cooked meal,

time for conversation, a few rollin laughs, someone sayin somethin
that takes me back to maybe Dallas or some other town, train whistles

or dark birds flyin, the rise of the breath, suddenly the loose heart.
To drive, load, clean. There are more lives than this plain desperation.

Look at the sandwich boards, think of the lives, the faces and hands
that promised action in the coat room at the end of a party,

the looks on the faces of those on the sidewalks, the dirt roads, the car
windows, anyone passin, the evenin he looked at me eager and avid

for a break out. The first time I drove with him I puked right on my dress
from the joy of speed. Yes I said let's just have everythin.

Suddenly tired, convinced it comes soon, I falter just briefly and all
the time in a purse I hid at his momma's house: the note he wrote callin me

the sweetest thing in all the world.

FIRST ARREST OF CLYDE BARROW AT AGE OF 8 YEARS

HOUSTON, TEXAS, MAY 26 —— AP ——
Perhaps the first warrant ever isssued for the arrest of the late Clyde Barrow, youthful robber and killer, has been found in the files at the courthouse here by J. W. Mills, clerk of the civil district courts.

The warrant was issued March 11, 1918, by Chester H. Bryan, former county judge, on complaint of R. R. Adcock, former chief proation officer. Barrow, then eight years old, was charged with being an incorrigible, with wandering the streets at night, and with burglarizing a house near his home.

Tried the next day in juvenile court, Clyde was sentenced to the Harris county school for boys for an indeterminate period. He remained there for two and one-half years.

T. G. Kenney, former superintendent of the school, said he considered Barrow "such a quiet and conservative youngster" that he brought him into his own home for a time to help take care of Mr. and Mrs. Kenney's baby.

The Shreveport Times, May 26, 1934

even the daylight lost its color

clouds bleach out like soda in a straw, my foot all cramp & gristle, time to stop the drivin, I've tore up these roads too long, looks like snow on treetops from the picker's cotton drift, went that way once: worthless

screech owl dips, bugs whine at my ear, blanket stinks of grease, someplace near lives comfort

blood smells like a gun before its oiled, snap that shut, close up your eyes too: sleep comes

Billy rode on a pinto horse
Billy the Kid I mean
And he met Clyde Barrow riding
In a little gray machine

Billy drew his bridle rein
And Barrow stopped his car
And the dead man talked to the living man
Under the morning star

— Bonnie Parker, from "Outlaws"

Acknowledgements

Go Down Together: The True Untold Story of Bonnie and Clyde by Jeff Guinn drew me to these characters, but it was the two first-person narratives, *My Life With Bonnie and Clyde* by Blanche Caldwell Barrow, and the interview with W. D. Jones, "Riding with Bonnie & Clyde" which originally appeared in *Playboy Magazine* in November 1968, that offered me the real voices I needed to hear.

I also drew material from the less reliable but fascinating account *The True Story of Bonnie and Clyde, as told by Bonnie's Mother and Clyde's Sister, Mrs. Emma Parker and Mrs. Nell Barrow Cowan*, compiled, arranged and edited by Jan I. Fortune; the novel *Hungry Men: The Story of a Tramp* by Edward Anderson; as well as the 1948 film *They Live By Night* (directed by Nicholas Ray), based on the Edward Anderson novel *Thieves Like Us*.

There is much available online, including film footage of Clyde Barrow's funeral and interviews with the posse. Whenever possible I drew exact newspaper reports from online archives.

I want to gratefully acknowledge the influence of John Dos Passos, to whom the title of the poem "camera eye" is a nod, as well as the extraordinary Elizabeth Stimpson who introduced me to his *USA* trilogy in 1968.

Many people helped with various aspects of this collection: Steve and Jenny Lapp were my companions on a ride in a beautiful 1934 Ford flathead v8 owned and driven at high speed down the back roads of Ontario by Donald Elliott; Donna Dixon and Dan Aykroyd drove me in Dan's Pierce-Arrow, the model that J. Edgar Hoover would have driven in as he imagined the hunt for Clyde Barrow. LuAnn Simpson, thank you for your encouragement all these years.

Tony Morphet and Ingrid de Kok introduced me to the work of photographer Roger Palmer. I am honoured to have his work on the cover of this book.

Thanks to Susan Werner for her song "The Last Words of Bonnie Parker" which influenced the poems profoundly.

Some of these poems have appeared in different forms in the following journals and anthologies: *Arc Poetry Magazine*; *Eleven Eleven*; *The Fox Chase Review*; *Ginosko Literary Journal*; *I Found It at the Movies: An Anthology of Film Poems*; *Pif Magazine*; *Poems from Planet Earth*; *PRECIPICe*; *PRISM international*; *The Society*; *Sugar Mule*; *Taddle Creek*; *This Magazine*.

I am grateful to my students past and present who have offered me so much and make me feel lucky to work with them, and to the Ontario Arts Council, the Canada Council for the Arts and the Queen's University Fund for Scholarly Research and Creative Work for their support.

Thank you to three very fine writers for their careful readings of the work: Diane Schoemperlen, superb literalist; to Anne-Marie Bennett, who clarified the structure, made me see the whole thing in new light and then introduced me to Sadiqa de Meijer, who became my literary coach and helpmeet extraordinaire.

A standing ovation to the people at Brick Books. I am enormously grateful to Kitty Lewis for her friendship and all she does for Canadian poets and poetry. It's always a pleasure to work with Alayna Munce, whose thoughtfulness and vigilance is much appreciated. Stan Dragland, your unwavering sense of language and attention to detail have added immeasurably to these pages.

When writing *Careen* I imagined my maternal grandfather, Harry Van Tress, who lived out his final years in Laredo, Texas and died, according to a lawyer, 'in penury'. He was a failed gunrunner. I never met him and wonder if he ever saw members of the Barrow Gang pass by.

Most importantly, thank you to my own dear gang, Daniel, Nicholas and Steffen, who have long since lit out for town, and always to Kenneth, my first reader and partner in crime, without whom the world would be a far less humorous and loving place.

CAROLYN SMART has written six previous collections of poetry, including *The Way to Come Home* (Brick Books, 1993), and *Hooked: Seven Poems* (Brick Books, 2009). Her memoir *At the End of the Day* (Penumbra Press, 2001) won first prize in the 1993 CBC Literary Contest. Smart is the founder of the RBC Bronwen Wallace Award for Emerging Writers and an editor for the Hugh MacLennan Poetry Series of McGill-Queen's University Press; since 1989 she has taught Creative Writing at Queen's University. She lives with her family in the country north of Kingston.